NURSING HOMES DON'T HAVE TO COST YOU EVERYTHING

The Seven Medicaid Mistakes to Avoid

Gregory P. Jimeno
ATTORNEY AT LAW

WORD ASSOCIATION PUBLISHERS
www.wordassociation.com
1.800.827.7903
TARENTUM, PENNSYLVANIA

Printed in the United States of America.

ISBN: 978-1-63385-479-6

Designed and published by

Word Association Publishers
205 Fifth Avenue
Tarentum, Pennsylvania 15084

www.wordassociation.com

1.800.827.7903

Table of Contents

PLANNING FOR THE INEVITABLE

When a family member (spouse, parent, aunt, or uncle) is admitted into a nursing home, it can be devastating for the entire family. First, there's the emotional component. Watching a loved one, who not too long ago was otherwise healthy, develop a sudden condition or illness that requires them to go into a nursing home can be hard to process. You want to be their caregiver but know you can't give them the round-the-clock care a nursing home can. This leaves the family with limited options. Although the nursing home is the last resort, it may become inevitable if their loved one continues to experience a decline.

Aside from the emotional toll on the family, there is a significant financial burden. Nursing home care is not cheap, and as we will discuss in the chapters to come, paying for the nursing home can take away all of the money that the family has saved during their lives. Not knowing where to turn or what options are available can often lead to not getting the appropriate care for your loved one and/or unnecessarily depleting their savings and investments - the two things you want to avoid at all costs!

HOW DO YOU DO THAT? BY PLANNING!

There are two stages in life when people can plan for nursing home care: The first and best time is well in advance of ever needing nursing home care. I discuss these advanced strategies in more detail in my book *How To Protect Your Home And Life Savings In Maryland*, which can be obtained by visiting www.ChesapeakeWillsAndTrusts.com. We call this pre-planning, as we seek to protect the home or other assets at least FIVE years before entering the nursing home.

The second opportunity people have to plan for nursing home care is when they have been admitted into the nursing home (commonly referred to as Medicaid Crisis Planning). We refer to this type of planning as *"crisis planning"* because the admission into a nursing home has created a crisis in terms of how to pay for care, including whether the person admitted into the nursing home should apply for Medicaid benefits.

Paying for the nursing home can take away all of the money that the family has saved during their lives

It is estimated that 70% of people aged 65 or above will need long-term care. **Based on this statistic, it is appropriate to say, the majority, if not all of you who are reading this, will have to develop a plan to**

pay for nursing home care. And some of you will need to conduct Medicaid Crisis Planning.

In Maryland, there are approximately 230 nursing homes that accept Medicaid. In those 230 nursing homes, there are roughly 30,000 nursing home beds available to be paid for by Medicaid. If a person is in a nursing home in Maryland, chances are, Medicaid is paying for their care.

THE QUESTION THEN BECOMES, WHAT STEPS NEED TO BE TAKEN TO GET QUALIFIED FOR MEDICAID?

Let's face it: Medicaid rules are difficult to understand even for professionals who deal with them on a daily basis. I receive calls from both current and potential clients telling me they have done their internet research and don't believe their loved one is eligible for Medicaid, according to the "information" they found on Google. As is often the case, the internet research led to the wrong conclusion about eligibility, leading to money being paid unnecessarily for a nursing home.

70% of people aged 65 or above will need long-term care.

Even judges find Medicaid rules tough to interpret. Courts have referred to Medicaid rules as "almost unintelligible to the uninitiated" and as an "aggravated assault on the English language, resistant to attempts to understand it."

Does this sound like something you want to go through alone, without legal help and guidance? Do you really want to rely on Google searches to protect your loved one's home and life savings? I know you don't, especially when there are options available that can help!

3 CHOICES

Paying for nursing home care can be overwhelming, but with the right knowledge and person in your corner, it doesn't have to be. There are three choices available that offer the assistance you and your loved ones desperately need. Here are your choices:

1. Private Pay
2. Long-term care insurance
3. Medicaid

First option: **Private Pay**. Private pay is ultimately paying out of pocket, and nursing home care isn't cheap! In our firm, we routinely deal with clients paying close to $15,000 PER MONTH for nursing home care. According to Genworth, the average cost of care for a private room in a nursing home in Maryland is scheduled to increase by 35% over the next 10 years and over 80% over the next 20 years! With average stays in the nursing home being measured by years - as opposed to days or months - most of a family's accrued wealth could be paid over to the nursing home.

Second option: **Long-term care insurance.** A standard long-term care policy will either pay the entire monthly nursing home bill or pay a portion to limit the out-of-pocket expense. When clients tell me they have long-term care insurance and aren't worried about depleting their resources to pay for the nursing home, I encourage them to check their long-term care policy to understand the payment terms. When long-term care insurance first came out, many of the policies provided up to 5 years of care for a generous monthly rate of pay. As time went on, the premiums of those policies increased. This reduced the coverage, and as a result, people who purchased policies that provided coverage for 5 years now had policies that only provided coverage for 2 or 3 years at a reduced monthly payment. The bottom line is just because someone has a long-term care policy does not mean they will have enough coverage to pay for the duration of their entire nursing home stay.

Third Option: **Medicaid**. Medicaid is long-term care insurance provided by the government and isn't available to everyone. It is a means-tested government program. In other words, the person applying for Medicaid must meet certain eligibility requirements, such as income and asset requirements.

For families with limited resources or who wish to leave an inheritance to the next generation, exploring whether Medicaid is an option to pay for their nursing home care is important. An initial review of the Medicaid qualifications could lead to a conclusion that the loved one in the nursing home would never be able to meet the strict financial qualifications for Medicaid. However, there are lawful ways to potentially become qualified for Medicaid without the nursing home resident losing their life savings.

Just because someone has a long-term care policy does not mean they will have enough coverage to pay for the duration of their entire nursing home stay.

Too often people make mistakes when trying to pay for nursing home care. In the chapters below, I will lay out some of the most common mistakes.

MISTAKE #1:

ASSUMING MEDICARE WILL PAY FOR LONG-TERM CARE IS A BIG MISTAKE

Right Way
Wrong Way

There are many things to deal with when a loved one enters a nursing home, and the shock of finding a way to make payments can be overwhelming. Many people wrongly assume that Medicare or Medicaid will automatically pay the monthly bill without regard to how different these programs operate. Before going any further, let's clarify: Medicare will not pay for long-term nursing home care.

Medicare is health insurance provided by the government. In order to receive Medicare, you must either be age 65 or older or have a disability, End-Stage Renal Disease, or ALS. Medicare has two parts: Part A provides hospital insurance, and Part B provides Medicare Insurance.

Medicare can provide limited coverage for a nursing home stay if the patient is admitted for "skilled nursing care." Think of skilled nursing care as rehabilitation services. Medicare will only pay up to 100 days of skilled nursing care and could cut off the payments during the 100-day period if Medicare determines that the received treatment is no longer necessary. If an additional stay in the nursing home is required, the patient must look at alternative payment options, potentially even paying out of pocket.

Let's use an example to highlight the differences between Medicare and Medicaid.

Jane is 85 and has been living at home with her spouse, Rob, who has been her primary caretaker since she was diagnosed with dementia. Rob had been able to provide for Jane until she fell and broke her hip. Jane would go on to spend time in a local hospital until she was transferred to a nursing home for physical therapy and rehabilitation. Because Jane was initially being provided rehabilitation services, Medicare provided payment to the nursing home.

However, on day 45, Medicare determined that Jane's rehabilitation was complete and that no additional therapy will improve her condition. Worse, Jane's dementia has advanced to the point that Rob could no longer provide the care she needed at home, resulting in Jane needing to stay in the nursing home.

Jane and Rob had a decision to make. They knew Medicare would no longer pay for Jane's care and there was the very real prospect that Jane and Rob's life savings may be needed to pay for her continued care in the nursing home. But instead of depleting their life savings, they begin exploring asset protection and appropriate spend down and asset protection strategies to make Jane financially qualified to receive Medicaid benefits.

Medicare will not pay for long-term nursing home care.

As you can see in the above example, qualifying for Medicaid can save you money when Medicare is no longer an option. But you first need to understand the rules of qualification.

MISTAKE #2:
MISUNDERSTANDING MEDICAID RULES CAN CAUSE DEVASTATING CONSEQUENCES

Right Decision
Wrong Decision

Medicaid can greatly reduce or, in some cases, even eliminate the private payment of the nursing home bill, but you need an understanding of its rules first.

There are several variations of Medicaid benefits, but this book is solely focused on the long-term care benefits available to nursing home residents. Failure to understand the qualification for Medicaid benefits could have a disastrous effect on your loved ones' life savings. Below are the criteria needed to become eligible for Medicaid benefits in Maryland:

1. You must be a citizen of the United States or have permanent residency
2. You must live in the State of Maryland
3. You must be medically qualified to receive nursing home care
4. Your monthly income must be below a certain limit
5. Your assets must be below a certain limit

This chapter will describe in detail the last two listed criteria – the criteria known as the income and asset tests. Let's start with the income test, which is the easiest of the tests to comprehend. If the cost of care is more than the monthly nursing home bill, the applicant meets the income test. Here's an example of the income test:

> *Peter is a nursing home resident and his nursing home bill is* ***$15,000*** *per month. Peter has a monthly income of* ***$5,000****, which is comprised of pension benefits and Social Security payments. Since Peter's nursing home bill is* ***GREATER*** *than his income, he meets the income test for Medicaid. If Peter meets the other qualifications for Medicaid, he will need to pay his monthly income to the nursing home and Medicaid would pay the balance.*

UNDERSTANDING MEDICAID ASSET RULES

The asset test is different depending on whether the Medicaid applicant is single or married. If the applicant is single, he or she can only have countable assets of **$2,500** in order to qualify for benefits.

The Medicaid asset rules for a married applicant are a bit more generous. The Medicaid rules aim to prevent the spouse living in the home (known as the Community Spouse) from losing all of his or her assets and permit him or her to keep some money to live on.

If the cost of care is more than the monthly nursing home bill, the applicant meets the income test.

At the time of writing this book, the community spouse can keep **$137,400**[1], while the spouse living in the nursing home can keep **$2,500**.

Aside from the additional amount of money the community spouse is permitted to keep, if the community spouse continues to reside in the family home, the value of the house is not counted in the **$137,400**. This means that the community spouse can keep the house AND an additional **$137,400**.

However, even with the increased asset limit for a community spouse and the exclusion of the family home, the asset test can be devastating for most families because the assets they worked so hard for their entire life could put them well over the Medicaid limit.

What assets are counted towards the asset limits listed above? Almost everything, although there are again some protections for married individuals. Take a moment to list out all of the assets of a loved one in the nursing home to see which are considered by Medicaid as available resources. Below is a list of categories of assets considered resources by Medicaid:

1. Bank accounts
2. Stocks

1) The $137,400 represents the Community Spouse Resource Allowance (CSRA) and is increased on a yearly basis

3. Bonds
4. Mutual Funds
5. IRA /401K/Other retirement accounts, even if there is a penalty for withdrawing the money
6. Cash value in life insurance policies
7. Motor vehicles
8. Motor homes
9. Boats

The above is **not** an exclusive list and is subject to some limited exclusions under the Medicaid laws, such as the marital house mentioned above if one spouse is still residing in the home. Because Medicaid counts nearly all of the assets of the person in the nursing home and the assets of their spouse, it is vitally important for the preservation of the assets to ensure you understand how those assets can be protected. That way, Medicaid qualification can be achieved without spending all of the family wealth paying for the nursing home bill.

One of the biggest areas of concern for most Medicaid applicants and their families is how retirement benefits (401k, IRA, 403b, etc.) are counted against a Medicaid applicant's asset qualification.

Peter, a nursing home resident, does not have a retirement account; however, his wife Sally, who resides in the marital home, had an IRA worth

$400,000. Although Sally is healthy and living at home, the entire balance of her IRA is a countable resource for Peter's nursing home qualification: subject to liquidation and being spent down. Thus, the amount of money in Sally's IRA alone puts Peter well over the Medicaid asset limit.

The major takeaway is that the assets of **BOTH SPOUSES,** even the healthy spouse living at home, may be forced into liquidation to help the spouse in the nursing home qualify for benefits.

With an understanding of the qualifications for Medicaid benefits, you are more likely to think you have all the tools you need to qualify. However, now comes the hard part… figuring out which strategies can be used to increase your loved one's chances of qualifying for Medicaid. The last thing you want is for your loved one to get penalized by your good intentions, whether by filing too early or by transferring assets improperly.

MISTAKE #3:
GIVING AWAY ASSETS IS A COSTLY MISTAKE

WRONG
WAY

If you think giving away the assets of the person in the nursing home just before filing the application is a proper strategy, you must immediately reassess your plan. The government does not allow this action and will impose a **MEDICAID PENALTY**.

THE MEDICAID PENALTY

The term Medicaid penalty sounds harsh, and it is. The government put the Medicaid penalty in place to prevent the giving away or gifting of assets to qualify financially for Medicaid right before filing an application.

Here is how the Medicaid application process works. When applying for benefits, Medicaid will review all financial information of the applicant over the past 5 years to determine if any assets were given away without fair compensation. This is called an "uncompensated transfer." If there are uncompensated transfers within the previous 5 years of entering a nursing home, Medicaid imposes a penalty.

So, how is the applicant penalized? Medicaid imposes a financial penalty on the applicant based on the amount of money gifted or given away. For every $10,000 given away within 5 years of entering the nursing home, Medicaid imposes a one-month ineligibility penalty. The $10,000 is referred to as the Medicaid divisor, which is set each year by the government. The amount of the gift is divided by the divisor and establishes the length of the Medicaid penalty. Here is an example:

> *Three weeks before going into the nursing home, Julia gives away $100,000 to bring her assets down to within the $2,500 Medicaid asset limit. If Julia were to immediately apply for Medicaid benefits, Medicaid would impose a 10-month penalty ($100,000 gift ÷ $10,000 divisor = 10 months). Although Julia is financially qualified for Medicaid because her assets are below the Medicaid asset limit, she is ineligible for 10 months of Medicaid benefits due to the penalty. The $100,000 Julia gave away would either need to be returned OR Julia would need to pay for her care through the end of the Medicaid penalty.*

People often confuse the IRS gift tax limit and the Medicaid penalty rules. The IRS permits a person to give away $16,000 per person, per year, without reporting the gift to the IRS. In fact, you can give away far more than $16,000 per person, per year, without paying gift taxes, although you may need to report the gift to the IRS. However, gifts to people that do not need to be reported to the IRS can still cause Medicaid penalties. For instance, if a mother were to give her 3 kids $10,000 each, the gift would not need to be reported to the IRS. However, if the mother enters a nursing home within 5 years of the gift, a Medicaid penalty of 3 months could be imposed for the combined $30,000 gift. If the nursing home costs $15,000 per month, mom would have to pay an additional $45,000 in nursing home costs as a result of the $30,000 gift. Thus a $30,000 gift has now turned into a $75,000 gift when factoring in the Medicaid penalty.

For every $10,000 given away within 5 years of entering the nursing home, Medicaid imposes a one-month ineligibility penalty.

So, what is considered a gift? The legal definition of a gift is: "a transfer or divestiture of ownership interest in assets owned by an applicant, recipient, or the individual's spouse for less than fair market value."

But when is a gift not a gift? In other words, when can you give a gift to someone without it being treated as an uncompensated transfer? Maryland law provides some insight on the certain types of transfers that might not be penalized if a Medicaid application is submitted. Here are a few examples:

1. The **gift was given not for the purposes of attempting to qualify for Medicaid** benefits. For instance, Sally gave $100,000 to her children 3 years ago. Sally, who was healthy at the time of

the gift, later had a sudden onset of a disability (stroke, heart attack, etc.) which necessitated her admission into a nursing home. Sally may be able to successfully convince Medicaid that the gift was not given in anticipation of entering a nursing home (3 years prior to admission while healthy) and that she did not need nursing home care UNTIL the sudden onset of a medical condition.

2. **Providing emergency financial aid to a family member.** The Medicaid applicant would need to show things such as eviction, shut-off notice, foreclosure notice, or even pleadings filed in bankruptcy court.

3. **Paying for medical or educational expenses** for family or close friends.

These are merely examples of how money given away within 5 years of entering the nursing home can be viewed by Medicaid as transactions for which a penalty should not be imposed. That said, it is generally best not to be in a position to have to explain why gifts were given, especially if a loved one is either about to go into a nursing home or has recently been admitted. In future chapters, we will discuss planning strategies that can be initiated if a loved one enters a nursing home.

It is generally best not to be in a position to have to explain why gifts were given.

THE CURE

What happens if there is a Medicaid penalty that is imposed from an uncompensated transfer? The Medicaid rules allow for the gift to be "cured." So, how does one cure a Medicaid penalty? It's simple - returning the money to the Medicaid applicant! Now, I recognize that returning the gift is often easier said than done. Once a gift is given, it is often spent, invested, or otherwise disposed of, especially gifts that were given years before the applicant entered the nursing home. However, for many of you reading this book, you have a loved one who has recently entered a nursing home and perhaps recently gifted a large sum of money in the hopes of applying for Medicaid benefits (before reading this chapter, of course!). If that is the case, a return of the money to the Medicaid applicant is the best way to cure the penalty so that other (more acceptable) planning options can be implemented. Maryland also permits a partial return of a gift, which will reduce the Medicaid penalty. If the recipient of a gift can only return $50,000 of the $100,000 gift, Medicaid will cut the Medicaid penalty in half, from 10 months with a $100,000 gift down to 5 months with a $50,000 gift after $50,000 is returned to the mother.

The bottom line is: don't gift! If you do give a gift, get it back! It can cause a period of ineligibility for Medicaid.

Maryland also permits a partial return of a gift, which will reduce the Medicaid penalty.

MISTAKE #4:
MAKING COMMON SPENDDOWN ERRORS

DO NOT
ENTER
WRONG
WAY

Now that we know gifting money is a huge mistake, we can now focus on how a proper spend down plan can help an applicant to qualify for Medicaid.

"Medicaid spend down" does not mean spending all of your loved one's money on the nursing home. This is so important I am going to repeat it. A Medicaid spend down does not mean spending all of your loved one's money on the nursing home! The law allows for assets above the Medicaid asset limit to be spent on items other than the nursing home bill. It is vitally important to Medicaid Crisis Planning that you understand what types of spend downs are permissible.

Far too often when I speak to a client, they tell me stories of watching their parents or loved one spend their entire life savings on the nursing home. Some clients even use the term "spend down" to refer to paying money to the nursing home. However, analysis of any Medicaid crisis case must start with the permissible spend downs.

While there are many permissible spend downs, we will focus on a few of the most commonly used and those that can have the most impact.

1. **Pay off any debts the Medicaid applicant may have.** Look for things such as credit card debt, car

debt, and even a mortgage. Many of these debts would survive after the death of the Medicaid applicant, so it makes sense to pay them with excess resources. Paying down these debts can only help to qualify for Medicaid but be sure to obtain current balances from any creditor of the Medicaid applicant before making the payments. Also, be sure to maintain an accurate record of both the debt and the payment.

2. **Make repairs to the home of the Medicaid applicant.** The home does not need to be in disrepair to spend money on repairs. For instance, the house may need an updated kitchen or bathroom, new windows, or a new roof. These are all perfectly allowable spend-downs, even if the Medicaid applicant can no longer return home and the repairs make the house more marketable for sale.

3. **The Medicaid applicant can pre-pay for his or her funeral.** But be careful - you want to make sure that the Medicaid applicant enters into an irrevocable funeral contract with a reputable funeral home. Most Maryland funeral homes have pre-printed forms that can create an irrevocable funeral contract. There is no limit to the amount that can be put into an irrevocable funeral contract.

4. **The cost of hiring an attorney to prepare a legal spend down and asset protection plan,** plus the preparation and filing of the application is an acceptable spend down. The cost of hiring an attorney to protect the life savings is often about the cost of a month or two of nursing home care. An attorney could potentially protect your loved one's life savings while greatly reducing the loved one's Medicaid bill!

> **Far too often when I speak to a client, they tell me stories of watching their parents or loved one spend their entire life savings on the nursing home.**

Spend downs are an important part of the overall Medicaid Crisis Plan, serving as an acceptable way to help an applicant get under the Medicaid limit. Here is an example of how the spend down plan can help prepare an applicant to qualify for Medicaid:

Louise is in the nursing home and attempting to qualify for Medicaid benefits; Louise, however, is $200,000 over the Medicaid asset limit. In reviewing her finances, Louise's family noticed that Louise had accumulated $20,000 in debt on various credit cards and owes another $5,000 towards unreimbursed medical care. Furthermore, Louise's house has been in disrepair for some time, so they *spend $155,000 for home repairs, including kitchen and bath remodeling, a new roof, and windows.*

After paying debts and home repairs, Louise is still $20,000 over the Medicaid asset limit. In order to complete her spend down, Louise enters into an irrevocable funeral contract for the $20,000. Louise has paid down her debt, spent money on repairing her house, and prepaid her funeral so her family is not later burdened with the cost. She is now eligible for Medicaid benefits.

The above example demonstrates how Medicaid spend down can be completed to secure the Medicaid asset qualification. You spend your assets on things for your benefit - debt, home repairs, prepaying your funeral, etc. - to become financially eligible for Medicaid.

Spend downs are an important part of the overall Medicaid Crisis Plan.

Next, we will discuss the types of strategies that can be implemented to protect your life savings and ensure that the nursing home bill is paid every month.

MISTAKE #5:
BELIEVING MEDICAID IS NOT AN OPTION

ONE WAY

You might find it difficult to believe that the title of this chapter is accurate, especially after I laid out the stringent asset and income requirements needed to qualify for Medicaid benefits. While it is true that Medicaid requires the applicant to have limited resources to receive benefits, nursing home residents do not need to lose all of their assets to receive benefits. There are ways to protect life savings even while qualifying for Medicaid.

It is not uncommon after someone is admitted into long-term care that a worker from the nursing home will inform the resident and family about the Medicaid asset limits. The resident will be offered assistance in preparing an application after the nursing home resident has spent any money he or she had over the Medicaid asset limit. Some residents may have years' worth of nursing home payments available in investments, bank accounts, and real estate. But since the workers at the nursing homes are not attorneys, they are not permitted to dispense legal advice on how to protect the residents' assets, even though there are several lawful and legal means available.

DON'T YOU WANT TO PROTECT YOUR LIFE SAVINGS AND PASS IT ON TO THE NEXT GENERATION WHILE QUALIFYING FOR MEDICAID BENEFITS?

When I speak with clients about their concerns when doing estate planning, nearly everyone is fearful of losing their home and life savings to nursing home costs. If a loved one is in a nursing home in Maryland, Medicaid is likely an option for paying the expenses. But what if someone is above the legal limits - how can that person apply for Medicaid benefits? This is when Medicaid Crisis Planning comes into play. Here are some basic strategies that can protect a loved one's assets while meeting the stringent Medicaid requirements:

1. Medicaid Compliant Annuity

Medicaid Compliant Annuities are most commonly used in cases where the applicant is married. Before we talk about specifics, it is important to note that the purpose of the Medicaid Compliant Annuity is to use any money the applicant has that is above the Medicaid asset qualification limit to purchase the annuity. The money used to purchase the annuity is returned to the community spouse in equal monthly payments.

The use of the Medicaid Compliant Annuity is absolutely permitted under State and Federal Medicaid rules. The government even goes so far as to ***establish strict guidelines*** for the terms and conditions of this annuity. Failure to comply with any of these requirements will make the money used to purchase the annuity a countable resource and/or create a Medicaid penalty and would destroy the purpose of the strategy. You should not purchase, or attempt to purchase, a Medicaid Compliant Annuity without first consulting with an Elder Law attorney.

Nearly everyone is fearful of losing their home and life savings to nursing home costs.

Keep this in mind when doing Medicaid Crisis Planning or when purchasing a Medicaid Compliant Annuity: the Medicaid Compliant Annuity is not a typical investment where one would shop around for the best rate of return. Many people are skeptical of investment vehicles, such as annuities, as part of their investment portfolio. The use of the Medicaid Compliant Annuity is for one purpose and one purpose only - to protect one's life savings. Your loved one in the nursing home could be faced with two choices: Pay the nursing home or purchase a Medicaid Compliant Annuity.

To purchase a Medicaid Compliant Annuity, one may need to liquidate investments such as stocks, mutual funds, and retirement accounts and these proceeds would be used to purchase the annuity. I understand that people become attached to investments they've owned for 20-30 years. However, these investments need to be liquidated at some point to pay for care or to conduct proper Medicaid Crisis Planning in order to protect the money. Let's take a look at an example of a married couple attempting to qualify for Medicaid:

Jane is in the nursing home, and she and her husband, Rob, are looking for ways to pay for her care. They have $500,000 worth of countable assets for Medicaid purposes. Next, we must determine how much money Rob and Jane are permitted to keep. Jane, as the nursing home resident, is entitled to keep $2,500 while Rob can keep $137,400, for a total of $139,900. When we subtract the amount of money Jane and Rob are permitted to keep from the number of their countable resources, we determine that they are $360,100 over the Medicaid asset limit.

The $360,100 of assets over the Medicaid limit get transferred to Rob. Rob then purchases a Medicaid Compliant Annuity with that $360,100. Once the annuity is purchased, Rob and Jane would be under the Medicaid asset limit, and Jane could apply for Medicaid benefits. If a 36-month annuity was purchased, Rob would receive nearly $13,000 per *month, while Jane's nursing home bill would be paid for by Medicaid.*

Instead of using their life savings to pay for the nursing home, Rob and Jane's life savings were used to purchase a Medicaid Compliant Annuity, and the purchase price of the annuity was returned over time to Rob.

The money used to purchase the annuity is returned to the community spouse in equal monthly payments.

2. Promissory Note

The use of a Medicaid Compliant Promissory Note is another planning technique most commonly used in crisis planning for a married couple. The assets of the above couple which exceed the Medicaid asset limit are transferred to the community spouse. The community spouse enters into a Promissory Note. In other words, the community spouse loans the amount of money over the Medicaid asset limit to a family member or another trustworthy individual. The terms of the Promissory Note would provide for equal monthly payments to be returned to the community spouse until the loan is repaid. Then the community spouse could keep the amount of the loan repayment (the assets of the couple that originally exceeded the Medicaid limit) to use as they see fit.

When considering using the Promissory Note, this is not an agreement you can write on the back of a napkin or have a handshake between kids and parents. The Promissory Note used for Medicaid purposes is highly regulated and must meet each requirement set out by the Medicaid rules. Let's take a look at an example:

> *Let's revisit Peter and Sally. Peter is in the nursing home and Sally is the community spouse. Peter and Sally have $500,000 in combined assets and have found themselves over the Medicaid limit by $360,100. Instead of purchasing a Medicaid Compliant Annuity, Sally enters into a promissory note with their son, John. The terms of the note provide that Sally will lend John $360,100, but John will repay that loan over the course of 3 years at a rate of nearly $13,000 per month until the note is repaid. The purpose is not necessarily to lend John money but to use the Medicaid Compliant Promissory Note as a way to protect the amount of money over the Medicaid limit while returning those funds to the community spouse.*

3. Gift and Return

This strategy is primarily used when trying to qualify a single applicant for Medicaid benefits. We know from prior discussions in this book that giving money away within 5 years of going into a nursing home can cause lengthy periods of Medicaid ineligibility;

however, at times, when qualifying someone for Medicaid benefits, we must give gifts to others in order to make sure all of the applicant's life savings are not being spent on nursing home care.

So, how do we use gifting as a strategy to protect assets? Maryland permits a partial return of gifted assets. This means that if money is given away from a Medicaid applicant's assets, the person who receives the gift does not need to return the entire gift in order for the applicant to qualify for Medicaid (many states require the entire gift to be returned, making this a state specific strategy). Only part of the gift must be returned to the nursing home to pay for the applicant's cost of care, and the remainder can be protected from nursing home costs.

Money away within 5 years of going into a nursing home can cause lengthy periods of Medicaid ineligibility.

Knowing how much of the gift can be kept and how much needs to be returned involves a complex series of factors that an experienced Elder Law attorney can assist with. Much like the discussion regarding Medicaid Annuities and Promissory Notes, there are several legal and practical factors to consider before entering into any of these strategies. There are many pitfalls to this strategy, and if not done correctly could adversely impact the Medicaid application.

Just know that all hope is not lost with a single Medicaid applicant. The applicant's life savings can be at least partially protected EVEN IF he or she is admitted into a nursing home, while getting Medicaid to pay for some or all of the nursing home bill. The best way to understand the "gift and return" strategy is through an example.

Ruth is single and has recently been admitted into a nursing home. At the time of her admission, she had $302,500 in countable assets. As a single applicant, Ruth is permitted to keep $2,500 of her assets, meaning that she is $300,000 above the Medicaid asset limit.

Ruth's daughter, Mary, is her financial power of attorney. Using a (properly drafted) financial power of attorney, Mary gifts herself the $300,000 of her mother's assets that are over the Medicaid limit, which leaves Ruth with the $2,500 allowable under the Medicaid rules.

Ruth can now apply for Medicaid benefits. Ruth is financially qualified EXCEPT for the $300,000 gift, which would create nearly a 30-month Medicaid penalty, during which time she would not be eligible for Medicaid benefits.

In consultation with an attorney, a gift and return strategy was designed. Assuming the nursing home's *bill is $15,000 per month, Mary would return $150,000, representing 10 months of payments, to the nursing home. The monthly payments to the nursing home would reduce the amount of the gift and, thus, reduce the length of the penalty. The penalty period would be cut in half and the remaining $150,000 can be retained by Mary. Ruth has now qualified for Medicaid while ensuring a significant portion of her life savings goes to her family and not toward her monthly bills.*

Let me provide a few words of caution on these above listed strategies: this is just a brief overview of asset protection concepts. DO NOT read this information and start planning on your own. Whether it is best to use a Medicaid Annuity or Promissory Note depends on the unique circumstances of each matter and determining which strategy works best requires thoughtful legal and practical analysis you can only get from an Elder Law Attorney.

MISTAKE #6:
APPLYING TOO EARLY OR TOO LATE

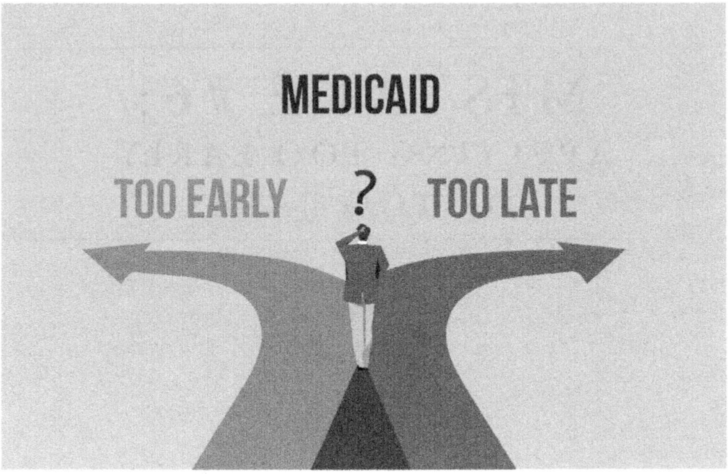
MEDICAID
TOO EARLY
?
TOO LATE

Timing is everything if you want to protect everything. Let's say you wish to file the Medicaid application - but is the timing right? In Medicaid Planning, there is a right and wrong time. Here are three timing mistakes you want to avoid:

1. Not filing an application
2. Filing an application too late
3. Filing an application too early

Any of these application mistakes could result in your loved one needlessly contributing more of his or her hard-earned money to nursing home care.

Let's look at the **first** timing error: never getting around to filing an application. Now that you are aware of Medicaid Crisis Planning strategies, it should be apparent now that if a loved one is in a nursing home you must explore the possibility of immediately implementing a Medicaid Crisis Plan to reduce the nursing home bill and protect your life savings. Consider yourself one of the lucky ones! Unfortunately, most people don't possess the knowledge you now do of these strategies and never fill out an application for Medicaid. It is a common problem that costs people everything.

The **second** mistake: filing too late. What does it mean to file "too late?" It means the applicant submits an application for Medicaid benefits after he or she has been financially eligible to receive benefits. As a result, they have spent more money on their nursing home care than they should have. This is a common issue I run across: People who could have protected their life savings but instead paid money to the nursing home, leaving little or nothing left for their beneficiaries.

> *Take, for example Peter, a nursing home resident, and his wife Sally, who is still living at home. Peter and Sally are unaware of the asset limit and continue to pay the full nursing home bill, even after their combined countable assets are below the Medicaid asset limit. Peter could have qualified for Medicaid benefits, but by being unaware that they were financially qualified, they, unfortunately, continued to spend their savings on the nursing home bill. Had Peter and Sally sought proper legal advice, they would have been able to protect their life savings while ensuring Peter received the care he deserved.*

Unfortunately, most people don't possess the knowledge you now do of these strategies.

Filing too late doesn't just mean filing after one is already eligible for benefits. Filing too late also means not taking advantage of appropriate spend down or asset protection strategies. Instead, filing too late could lead to money being spent on care that could have been saved or otherwise protected from the nursing home bill. Failing to take advantage of protection planning while continuing to pay full nursing home bills is a mistake too many people make.

If not filing an application is bad and filing an application too late is bad, you may be asking, "Is it best to just file an application for Medicaid when your loved one immediately enters the nursing home?" The answer is NO!

This leads us to the **third** filing error: filing too early. It's not uncommon for a Medicaid application to be filed by the nursing home or a helpful family member immediately after the loved one is admitted into a nursing home. However, the problem is that the vast majority of those initial applications will get denied, as the applicant is not yet qualified for Medicaid benefits. If the applicant is over the resource limit and the application is denied, it may impact the applicant's ability to protect their assets. The best rule to follow when submitting a Medicaid application is not to file unless the applicant is financially qualified. This means the applicant is either below the resource limit or has successfully completed a spend down and/or asset protection plan. **Never**, under any circumstances, should you file an application without knowing the rules, only for it to be denied. Instead, get the proper legal advice you need so there is no question your application will be approved when your time to file comes.

If the Medicaid applicant or his or her spouse has gifted money within 5 years of applying for Medicaid benefits an application filed too early could lead to an unnecessary penalty being imposed. Let's take a scenario where a Medicaid applicant made an uncompensated transfer (gift) of $300,000 4 years and 6 months prior to needing nursing home care. We know from our earlier discussions that this gift would likely lead to a 30-month penalty. Under Medicaid law, the penalty begins not from the time of the gift but rather from the date of the application. If an application were to be filed at the time of admission into the nursing home, there would be a 30-month penalty imposed; as a result, the Medicaid applicant would have to pay for 30 months of care out-of-pocket. However, if the Medicaid applicant received proper legal advice, he or she would have known to private pay for the nursing home for 6 months before submitting the application. At that point, the gift would have been given more than 5 years before the filing of the application and no penalty would apply!

MISTAKE #7:
GOING AT IT ALONE WITHOUT AN ELDER LAW ATTORNEY

Throughout this book I have tried to explain legal strategies and techniques to help educate you about ways to help pay for nursing home care without losing everything, and I hope it serves you well. In my experience talking to many clients and prospective clients over the years, the most common mistake people make is failing to protect their assets because they fail to get legal advice. Families have needlessly emptied their loved one's life savings and bank accounts and sold the family home to pay for care that could have been paid for by Medicaid.

Unfortunately, many assumptions are made when it comes to paying for the care of a loved one in a nursing home; Some people believe their loved one will never qualify for Medicaid and need to pay out of pocket, and others think their loved one will receive substandard care if they receive Medicaid. Even worse, some children believe that they need to pay out of their own pocket to pay for their parents nursing home care. All of these beliefs are false. Even though the Medicaid asset limits are low (and extremely low for a single applicant), all hope isn't lost to protect one's life savings if someone enters a nursing home.

Properly trained elder law attorneys can be of great assistance in helping a nursing home resident apply for Medicaid, even if the applicant had done little to no estate planning prior to entering the nursing home. But it is certainly more beneficial to have a proper estate plan in place.

SO WHAT EXACTLY CAN AN ATTORNEY DO TO HELP?

Provide Guidance - Money is almost always a factor in determining where a loved one should reside. Some families will decide that a loved one is better served in a nursing home that does not accept Medicaid, and they will private pay using the nursing home resident's assets. Since the vast majority of nursing homes in Maryland accept Medicaid, it is likely that help could be available to reduce the monthly bill the nursing home resident is required to pay. Lastly, some families are hesitant to put their loved ones in a nursing home, where they would get the care they need, believing that they will lose the nursing home resident's life savings. Knowing that there is financial help available to ensure proper care without losing all of their loved one's life savings is often a big relief for families and makes sure that the loved one gets the care that he or she deserves.

Review assets - No Medicaid Crisis Plan can be completed until there is a complete gathering and review of the applicant's assets. A complete review consists of current bank statements, real estate holdings, real estate values, and the like. It also requires an analysis of five years' worth of the applicant's financial history. Remember, Medicaid will look back five years to see if any assets were disposed of for less than fair market value and impose a penalty. Knowing this information and conducting a thorough review is vitally important.

Develop & implement a protection plan - Once it is determined that Medicaid can reduce the monthly nursing home bill and assets are thoroughly reviewed, an elder law attorney will help to develop a plan to qualify for Medicaid while ensuring the protection of the applicant's home and life savings.

Prepare & file the application- Once a crisis plan is implemented, an elder law attorney will prepare and submit the application. The attorney will ensure that all proper documentation is submitted to the state, including the financial statement, real estate deeds, and affidavits from people with knowledge of the applicant's financial or personal affairs.

Properly trained elder law attorneys can be of great assistance in helping a nursing home resident apply for Medicaid.

With all that said, the most important job of an attorney is to listen to the unique needs of each family and situation. This is not an opportunity to prove how smart he/she is or use big legal terms to try and impress. Our job is to simply listen. Only then can we offer our clients the best possible advice that is fitting to their personal situation.

Do you have the legal and emotional fortitude to fill out a Medicaid application without assistance from a professional who is trained in protecting your home and life savings?

ABOUT THE AUTHOR

A lifelong resident of Maryland, Gregory P. Jimeno is a recognized leader in the legal community. Mr. Jimeno has been assisting clients with their estate planning needs for close to 20 years. He is a member of the Estate and Trust Law Section of the Maryland State Bar Association and the National Academy of Elder Law Attorneys. He is a founder of Chesapeake Wills And Trusts, which is dedicated to estate planning and elder law. Mr. Jimeno is a selected SuperLawyer - a distinction only given to the top 10% of lawyers in the state - in the area of estate planning and is recognized as a Leading Lawyer in Estate Planning and Elder Law by "What's Up Annapolis?" magazine.

Mr. Jimeno has been committed to supporting families in protecting their assets and safeguarding their futures after seeing first-hand the impact improper planning can have on a family. His grandparents established a plan they thought would protect their assets and themselves from the inevitable high cost of nursing home care just to find out the estate planning tools they relied upon weren't protecting them as well as they could have. This is the nightmare Mr. Jimeno works to help families avoid.

Over the years, Mr. Jimeno has also become a sought-after speaker on the topics of estate planning and elder law. As the author of the book *How To Protect Your Home And Life Savings In Maryland*, he has shared his experiences in estate planning to help others properly put plans in place to make things easier on their families upon their death or disability. It's safe to say, in the 20 years he has devoted to helping families protect their assets and safeguard their futures, Gregory P. Jimeno has made a lasting impact on his local community.

WA

Made in the USA
Monee, IL
04 November 2026

67381819R10039